AF515639

# RAWER

Ninko Kirilov

Copyright© 2023 Ninko Kirilov
ISBN: 978-81-19228-15-7

First Edition: 2023
Rs. 200/-

***Cyberwit.net***
HIG 45 Kaushambi Kunj, Kalindipuram
Allahabad - 211011 (U.P.) India
http://www.cyberwit.net
Tel: +(91) 9415091004
E-mail: info@cyberwit.net

No part of this book may be reproduced or transmitted in any form or by any means, electronic, mechanical, photocopying, or otherwise, without the express written consent of Ninko Kirilov.

# Contents

# VENI

# BEFORE BREAKFAST

I love it when we're honest before breakfast.
everyone has the breath of himself
and toothpaste.
everyone still smells like his nightmares.
if you're honest before breakfast
you'll learn who you desire the most.

# PORTRAIT

you're just the opposite of 200 snowdrops.
you have dirt under the nails.
you walk like a child.
you never know the names of your relatives.
and you don't have a name
to suit you.
you don't strike poses.
you show through.
you yawn often.
you smoke only after eating
and after smoking you drink.
you have at least a five-line
on your forehead.
and you expect the violas
to explode in your ears
like 200 snowdrops
without any green and white.

# PAPERCLIP

kiss
until something bends.

***

spend more time with her.
spend more time with her.
wake up half an hour before her in the morning
and watch her.
send her to work.
make a breakfast in bed for her.
drink some coffee with her.
make her coffee
that she'll never forget.
drink wine with her -
let it be by your choice
and never tell her what it is.
make sandwiches for her.
send her pictures of you.
nothing will ever wait for you.
never,
never,
never ever
apologize to yourself and her.
give her a chance
to see you.
her mind will be a camera.

# DINNER

sashimi and love -
as if you have turned a man inside out
and you kiss him.

# ABSOLUTELY LOGICAL

a Komodo dragon absolutely logical started to think
what would it be
if he was a human:
he would have to put on clothes,
go to work,
communicate with other people,
use money,
have a family.

then the Komodo dragon
saw a duck,
ate it
and absolutely logical started to think
what would it be
if he was duck.

# CHERRY ZADUSHNITSA

children eat cherries on my grave
and spit the cherry stones.
they plant a tree
to keep me a shadow.

* a traditional Christian holiday which is in memory of all souls which go back after Maundy Thursday before Easter

***

I don’t hear anyone to call me.
however I lift up the receiver.
I say hello.
I hear back hello.

***

drink a pill
to sleep.
drink a pill
not to sleep.
drink a pill
not to think about her.
drink a pill
not to dream of her.
and you'll never know
which one is the dream,
which one is the reality.
never cry in your sleep.
just don't.
for me.
drink a pill.
everything is going to be all right.
if it doesn't work
there are other pills.

# HAZARD

sometimes you have to bet on the losing horse
without hoping for a win.
you bet
and you know you're going to lose.
when you order an expensive Champagne
you don't complain about the acid reflux later.

# RACHMANINOV

he never says
"see you"
because he never knows
if we'll see each other again.
he always says
"let God be with you"
because he really means it
and
"let God be with you"
sounds like
a second piano concert.

# NOTE TO SELF

don't forget:
the heart has two valves.
the directions are four.

# IF YOU WERE AN ANGEL

if you were an angel
you wouldn't ask anyone
how are you
but yourself
how am I.

# ANGEL

the girl dreams that everything is christmassy.
not only the mood
but everything.

white.

and red.

the girl walks out on the terrace.
cuts her wrists with a smile.

and jumps christmassy into the snow.

# DEVOLUTION 2

I can’t swim.
I throw myself from the bridge.
wings grow on my back.
I eat them.
I sink.
gills grow on my neck.

# THE FISH

something hollows us
and it needs some bait.
a black bait
by manure worms
so the fish to get caught
on our pain,
on those of our days,
on the dirty summer,
on the pretty streets,
on the brave tears.

the fish
that we ate,
that we forgot,
that we gave birth to,
with which we swam.
and the fish
which are silent in the waters
of our lives.
darling,
turn me into a fish,
caress me with scales.

because we don't always see
what disgusts us
in them,
in us -
wet,
flabby,

without shells,
little, funny drowning men,
who forget to swim
and still draw
the face of God.

# VIDI

# LEAVING LAS VEGAS

the first bar
where they know what you drink
and you don't have to order -
that's your Las Vegas.

that place
where you secretly poor
cheap liquor in your tea -
that's your Las Vegas.

someone's home
where you go for the first time
and then throw up from the terrace -
that's your Las Vegas.

the panic attack at night,
the look to see if your cellphone and wallet
are on their places -
that's your Las Vegas.

the feeling
that you're going to die
on a bench on the main street
and have noone to call to -
that's your Las Vegas.

and then comes that thought:
there is only one woman
to think about

and if you had lost her
you're always going to look for
someone like her.
she is your Las Vegas.

# WE FORBID

we forbid
vodka with black currant.
it's just like to lick
a rusty rail
and the wash your mouth
with medicine alcohol.

we forbid
vodka with mango.
it's just like an egg shell -
you chew it
and there's nobody
to freshen your lips.

we forbid
vodka with pineapple -
a very dumb fruit
especially on a pizza.

we forbid
vodka without a sour cherry.
we've said it before -
the sour cherry can break a tooth
and a vodka without a sour cherry stone
is like vodka without vodka.

# A CONCERTO FOR VODKA, HASHISH AND SALIVA PERFORMED BY ANITA PALLENBERG

she arranges word after word
in a chromatic scale,
in tones and semitones,
in moans and semimoans.
then she laughs in a scorching crescendo.
she kisses staccato.
a metronome tongue.
allegro vivace.

# DRESS / ROLE

she stand near the bed.
her cell phone rings:

- yes, darling,
I'm coming.
sorry for being late.

she puts on her dress without any underwear.
(she never took off her shoes.)

she is going to the next play.

# THE DRESS

if you cut yourself
at least try to leave a stain
either on some wear,
or on your mind.

the edge of her dress
is sharp
and if you're not a skillful rope walker
you may fall
and fall
and fall
and continue falling
until she catches you.

you may grow flowers
or have a cat
or a kid.
but you can also don't do it,
don't try it.
years later you'll think
what would happen
if you have reached out
to her dress.

and if you had cut yourself
would it leave a stain
either on some wear,
or in her mind.

## THE DRESS 2

she could fit in it again.
miscarriage.

# TO REACH THAT POINT

you cut off your buttons,
you'll sew them again.
your stuff wear themselves alone.
that exact couch -
you will write me from there.
you gather the leaves in a pile
and I harvest them.
there's no more coffee.
you kiss by habit,
you don't remember how long
there are no flowers at your home.
your shoes are walking by themselves.
you go to see a new place to rent.

it hurts up to hurt.
it hurts up to nothing.
people nail children's coffins.

# HIS SON DIED AT A CAR ACCIDENT

that's what they told him.
at first he screamed.
he howled.
he cried.
and again
he screamed,
he howled
and he cried.
then he started drinking.
with every glass his son
became more and more not dead.
closer.
here -
one more
and he is almost
holding his neck
instead of a glass.

he wants to kill him
so to continue with his drinking.

# TUESDAY GLASS

I'll never drink again.

I pour myself some.

never again.

someone comes to visit me.
brings a bottle.
then leaves.

then I leave.

# COLD TURKEY

I learned how to run vertically
and to shave myself in sand
instead of a mirror.

# 2018

I measure my veins with a measuring line.
I draw bridges over them.
I cross them just in half.
the bed is half empty.
half of the night I dream of end points,
half of the night I can't sleep endlessly.

I draw some bridges
just to jump from them.

# ALMOST

I peel and cut potatoes.
I cut my thumb.
I swear.
I color the potatoes in pink.
(my pink period.)
I cook.
I serve.

it's great,
you say.
you did your best.

the sky under your eyes is blue.
(your blue period.)

not my best,
I say.
almost my best.

# BULLFIGHT

some bull calls me every night
at 3 or 4.
he wakes me up
doesn't say a thing
and listens to me breathing.
that's why I keep quiet.

that bull could be no bull at all.
could be a woman.
or a future version of me.
or you.
or some woman's child
that I have forgotten in the hurry.

the bull knows:
the phone is a magenta cape.

I know:
all bulls are color-blind.

# BINGO LINE

women's voices read the numbers.
new telephone numbers of people
to fall in love in.
but nobody writes them down.

a powder as white as your hair falls down.

take out your credit card -
they announced a line.

# AMAVI

# CIRCLE

you are a Ferris wheel.
at first we're up,
then down.
you capture every visitor in a cabin.
I use you as a frisbee
and throw you over that meadow.
there are no dogs
to chase you.

I run to you.
I turn you into a coin
and put you into a coffee vending machine.
it doesn't want you.
I still want some caffeine
but I put you in my pocket.

I use you as a potter's wheel.
I make a pot.

Picasso says:
if you want to create a woman
first you have to hold her tight by the throat.

## THE GIRL WITH THE STRANGE YES

she covered herself in cotton candy.
I wasn't hungry.
she poured some cherry juice on herself.
I drank vodka.
she made my bed.
I slept on the floor.
I invited her to lie down next to me.
she answered with a distinctly NO.

# PETRICHOR

the scent after the rain
reminds me of
the scent after you.
but after the first one
my face is dry.

# CORRESPONDENCE

I write to you with a pencil,
a chalk,
a charcoal from that fire,
a brick,
a colorful dust for a mandala.

you can erase everything.

write to me with a rubber,
invisible ink,
the edge of the last coin,
soil.

I can write you a letter
written as if it's from you.
and even better -
as if it's from someone else.

# SHE WRITES

every woman is an orgy:
many women and men have sex inside of her.
she writes.

# A LONG GOOD MORNING NOTE

if you wake up before me
eat all the tulips.
I left a whole vase near the window.

water the other flowers.
Feed the cat-dog.

don't forget to call me
if you remember
that today I'm getting 92 years.

pour me something
at least 1/5 of my age.
let it be in a crystal glass.

I'll call you in the afternoon.
try to sound casual.

buy yourself a new pen.
that one doesn't do.

# ABSURDS

if you had red shoes
you'd be taller.
if you had more jigsaw puzzles
you'd arrange them.
if you'd live 7 kilometers away from me
you'd have more jigsaw puzzles.
if you haven't had me
you'd have red shoes.
A MEMORY BOX

you fold and you put in.
things,
gestures and words.

all of them whisper to you
possibilities.

artifacts of a novel.
still unwritten.

it could be scary beautiful.
it could be just scary.

# MATHEMATICS

I gather
hats,
swears,
old magazine issues.

she gathers
crab skulls,
melted wax in her hands,
burned out matches.

I take out
my glasses,
money for the bill,
some joke of ours.

she takes out
all good in me,
all bad in me,
all
and the change.

* * *

I cry
only when I cut onions.

I cut onions
only when you're not around.

# HEAVY WEIGHT

holding one wedding ring
in each of his giant fists
he cries
and swings.

# WHEN YOU SLEEP IN THE NEXT ROOM

is a night.
but not quite.

you breathe air as my own.
but not quite.

you sleep in a bed like ours.
but not quite.

you have a body.
I can touch you.
but not quite.

you can tell me something
and you almost want to.
but not quite.

you love me.
but not quite.
quite not.

# STACCATO

midlife crisis.
middle finger
and a middle class.
the middle pyre is still young.
it fires only by that cigarette.
there's no middle ground, nothing's a middle.
everyone live in extremes,
everyone is sick.
please,
meet me somewhere in the middle.
the winter freshens up to a summer,
watered down softly,
staccato softly.

softly.

crippled.

as your dreams are.

www.ingramcontent.com/pod-product-compliance
Lightning Source LLC
Chambersburg PA
CBHW050026170726
48282CB00025B/562
*9788119228157*